Tulika

The Seed

बीज

Deepa Balsavar

दीपा बलसावर

Hindi by Tara Kaushal

For Tara and Kannagi
Nishant, Tanay, Tanay and Teesta
Chaitanya, Anandi and Niranjan
Aditya, Rika and Zaid
Rajat, Manasa and Sambhavi

The Seed / Beej (English-Hindi)
ISBN 81-8146-110-X
© Deepa Balsavar
© Dual language text Tulika Publishers
First published in India 2005

Published by
Tulika Publishers, 13 Prithvi Avenue, Abhiramapuram, Chennai 600 018, India
email tulikabooks@vsnl.com   *website* www.tulikabooks.com

Printed and bound by
Rathna Offset Printers, 40 Peters Road, Royapettah, Chennai 600 014, India

www.tulikabooks.com   For more information about Tulika or to order books visit our website.

I found a seed.

मुझे एक बीज मिला।

I put it in a pot.

मैंने उसको गमले में डाला।

I gave it water and
lots of sunshine.

मैंने उसे पानी दिया
और बहुत सारा धूप।

Is it a tree?

क्या यह पेड़ है?

Is it a Bush?

क्या यह झाड़ी है?

Will it have flowers?

क्या इसमें फूल होंगे?

Will it have fruit?

क्या इसमें फल होंगे?

Will it grow tall?

क्या यह लम्बा ऊँचा होगा?

Will it stay small?

क्या यह छोटा ही रहेगा?

I dont know.

मुझे नहीं पता।

It doesn't matter!

कोई फ़र्क नहीं पड़ता!